Contents

1 Dropping the Bomb

On 6 August 1945, Dr Michihiko Hachiya woke on a fine morning in his house in Hiroshima, a city on the island of Honshu in the south of Japan. He wrote in his diary: 'The hour was early, the morning still, warm and beautiful.'

Japan had then been at war with the United States and its allies for three and a half years. The war was going very badly for Japan and most Japanese cities had been devastated by American bombing raids. But Hiroshima, a port and industrial centre with a population of around 300,000, had been largely untouched by the bombing. The city was the headquarters of Japan's 2nd Army and more than 40,000 soldiers were stationed there. But the great majority of the population were women, children and old people, because the men were away fighting.

On that fine summer morning Hiroshima bustled with packed trams trundling through busy streets and soldiers performing their daily physical exercises outside their barracks. There had been an air-raid

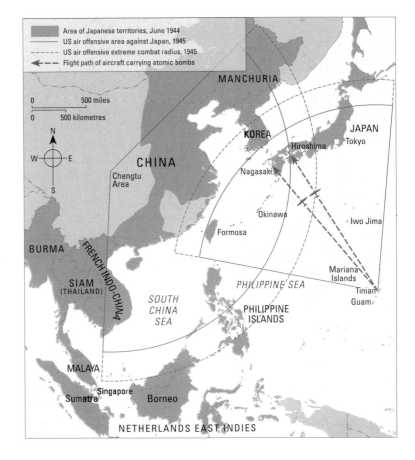

In 1941-42 Japan conquered a large area of Asia and the Pacific. The United States and its allies fought back and captured the Mariana Islands, including Tinian, in the summer of 1944. This brought Japan within range of American B-29 bombers, which had devastated many Japanese cities in a sustained air offensive by the time atomic bombs were dropped on Hiroshima and Nagasaki in August 1945.

HOW DID IT HAPPEN ?
HIROSHIMA

R. G. Grant

FRANKLIN WATTS
LONDON•SYDNEY

First published in 2005 by Franklin Watts
Reprinted 2007

Copyright © 2005 Arcturus Publishing Limited

Franklin Watts
338 Euston Road, London, NW1 3BH

Franklin Watts Australia
Level 17/207 Kent Street, Sydney, NSW 2000

Produced by Arcturus Publishing Limited
26/27 Bickels Yard, 151–153 Bermondsey Street
London SE1 3HA

Series concept: Alex Woolf
Editor: Philip de Ste. Croix
Designer: Stonecastle Graphics
Picture researcher: Thomas Mitchell

Picture credits:
All the photographs in this book were supplied by
Getty Images and are reproduced here with their
permission. The photographs appearing on the pages
listed below are Time Life images.
Time Life Pictures/Getty Images: 28, 30.

A CIP catalogue record for this book is available
from the British Library

Dewey Decimal Classification Number: 940.54'25

ISBN: 978-0-7496-7722-0

Printed in China

Franklin Watts is a division of
Hachette Children's Books

Colonel Paul Tibbets waves to news photographers from the cockpit of his B-29 bomber before taking off on the mission to drop the atom bomb on Hiroshima. Tibbets had the name Enola Gay painted on the aircraft the day before the flight.

warning at 7.15, but nothing had happened and the all-clear followed. An hour later, few people paid much attention as three high-flying American bombers appeared glinting silver in the blue sky over the city.

The bombers were B-29s from Group 509 of the US Army Air Force. They had taken off from their base on Tinian Island in the Marianas at 2.45 a.m. local time, embarking on a 2,400-km flight across the Pacific Ocean. Their mission was to drop the first atom bomb – a device thousands of times more destructive than any previously used in the history of warfare.

Vital Mission

The atom bomb was in an aircraft commanded by the commander of Group 509, Colonel Paul W. Tibbets. He had named the bomber Enola Gay, his mother's maiden name. The bomb had been developed in total secrecy, and even when they took off most of the Enola Gay's

12-man crew still did not know all the facts about the device they were carrying. But they did know that they had embarked on a vital mission to drop a bomb of massive explosive power. They had been told that, if successful, the bomb would force Japan to surrender.

The flight to Hiroshima was uneventful. By this time in the war, Japan had almost no air defences left. The major risk to the bombing mission was the weather. The attack had to be carried out from high altitude, because otherwise the mighty explosion would destroy the aircraft. But the ground had to be visible for the bomb to be dropped accurately. If it was cloudy, the mission would be aborted. Three other B-29s had been sent ahead to report back on weather conditions over

The Boeing B-29 Superfortress was the most advanced bomber aircraft of its day, the only type then capable of flying the distance from Tinian Island to Japan and back. Despite its four powerful engines, it had difficulty taking off with the atom bomb – weighing 4.4 tonnes – on board plus a full fuel load for the long journey.

VOICES FROM THE PAST
View from the air

Sergeant Robert Caron, the tail gunner on the Enola Gay, recalled what he saw after the bomb exploded:

'*The mushroom [cloud] itself was a spectacular sight, a bubbling mass of purple-gray smoke and you could see it had a red core in it and everything was burning inside… I saw fires springing up in different places, like flames shooting up on a bed of coals… It looked like lava or molasses covering the whole city, and it seemed to flow outward up into the foothills … so pretty soon it was hard to see anything because of the smoke.*'

Quoted in Richard Rhodes, *The Making of the Atomic Bomb* (Penguin, 1986)

Japan – it was one of these aircraft that triggered the early air-raid warning in Hiroshima that day. They radioed Tibbets the news that bombing conditions at Hiroshima were perfect.

The Enola Gay approached its target flying at 320 km/h at a height of 9,500 metres. The aiming point was the Aioi Bridge in the centre of Hiroshima. One minute from the target, Tibbets ordered the crew to put on polaroid goggles to protect their eyes. At 8.15 local time the bomb was released. Tibbets put the B-29 into a sharp turn, struggling to put the maximum distance between the aircraft and bomb by the time it exploded. A minute after it was dropped, the atom bomb airburst over the city.

After the first shock waves had passed, the crew looked back at Hiroshima and saw the city, in Tibbet's words, 'hidden by that awful cloud … boiling up, mushrooming and incredibly tall.' The airmen had been eager to carry out an important task, and part of their immediate reaction was satisfaction that the mission had been accomplished successfully. Radar officer Lieutenant Jacob Beser recorded that his first thought was: 'What a relief it worked.' The B-29s flew back to Tinian, where the airmen received a hero's welcome.

Flight and ground crew pose for cameras at Tinian airfield after the successful dropping of the bomb on Hiroshima by the Enola Gay. There was a sense of satisfaction and relief that the mission had gone smoothly.

Utter Devastation

The effect of the bomb on Hiroshima was utter devastation. It began with an intense flash of light and heat lasting less than second. In that brief moment, thousands of people near the point of the explosion died, burned to a cinder or totally vaporized. All that was left of some of them was a shadow on a wall. Further from the centre of the explosion, tens of thousands were blinded by the flash or suffered terrible burns. The flash was followed by a blast wave that destroyed almost every building in an area of 12 square kilometres. Splinters of shattered glass and wood were driven deep into people's bodies by the force of the blast. Many were buried under rubble as buildings collapsed.

After the explosion the sky was black with dust and debris. Violent winds swept the city, setting up firestorms that flared unpredictably, trapping masses of victims attempting to find some refuge from the catastrophe. Hiroshima's waterways were filled with the bodies of those who had jumped in to escape the fires or to cool their intolerable burns and had drowned.

VOICES FROM THE PAST

'A shattering flash filled the sky...'

One survivor of the Hiroshima bombing was Futaba Kitayama. She later recalled the moment the bomb exploded:

'*...a shattering flash filled the sky. I was thrown to the ground as the whole world collapsed around me ...I couldn't see anything. It was completely dark... All the skin came off my face, and then all the skin on my arms and hands fell off. The sky was black as night, and I ran homewards towards the Tsurumi River bridge. People by the hundreds were flailing in the river...*"

Stephen Harper, *Miracle of Deliverance* (Sidgwick & Jackson, 1985)

Hiroshima after the bombing: about 70,000 of the 76,000 buildings in the city were damaged or destroyed. Local doctor Michihiko Hachiya recorded: 'Nothing remained except a few buildings of reinforced concrete... For acres and acres the city was like a desert except for scattered piles of brick...'

Dr Hachiya, badly injured, staggered through the city in search of medical help. His diary records horrors such as victims whose 'eyes, noses and mouths had been burned away' so that you could not tell the front of their heads from the back. People wandered the streets with burned skin hanging from their bodies, desperately searching for aid of some kind. Soon, a sinister black rain began to fall over the city.

The Human Cost

Three days after the dropping of the atom bomb on Hiroshima, a second atom bomb was dropped on the city of Nagasaki. Five days later, Japan surrendered. Thousands of soldiers waiting to enter battle or prisoners of war starving in Japanese camps believed that the bomb had ended the war and saved their lives. British wartime leader Winston Churchill described it as 'a miracle of deliverance'.

But the human cost in the devastated cities was immense. No one knows exactly how many people died as a result of the Hiroshima bombing. Immediately after the war it was estimated that about 80,000 people died either as a result of the heat flash and blast, or from exposure to gamma radiation released by the explosion, which killed victims in 20 to 30 days. The Hiroshima city government, however, claims that the true death toll was 140,000 by the end of 1945, with thousands more subsequently dying of the long-term effects of radiation.

Survivors of the bombing, suffering from burns and lacerations, take shelter in one of the makeshift hospitals that were set up in damaged buildings. Most of Hiroshima's medical personnel were themselves killed or wounded in the bombing. The few surviving doctors had no way of treating the radiation sickness of which their patients soon began to die.

HOW DID IT HAPPEN?

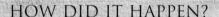

Morality and the bomb

In an article entitled 'Thank God for the Atom Bomb', published in 1981, author Paul Fussell defended the bombing of Hiroshima as necessary to save American soldiers' lives. In 1945 Fussell had been a young soldier preparing to fight in an invasion of Japan. When he and his fellow soldiers heard the news of the Hiroshima bombing, Fussell wrote, 'we cried with relief and joy. We were going to live.'

In response to Fussell's article, Professor Michael Walzer denounced the use of the atom bomb as totally immoral. He wrote: 'The bombing of Hiroshima was an act of terrorism… The goal was to kill enough civilians to shake the Japanese government and force it to surrender. And this is the goal of every terrorist campaign.'

For his part, Enola Gay pilot Colonel Tibbets never wavered in his attitude to the bombing, stating almost half a century after the event: 'I had no problem with it. I know we did the right thing…'

Paul Fussell and Michael Walzer, *The New Republic* magazine (1981); Paul Tibbets quoted in an interview with Studs Terkel, *The Guardian* (2002)

2 War Without Limits

The dropping of the atom bomb on Hiroshima occurred during the final stages of the most destructive war in human history – the Second World War. An estimated 50 million people had already died in the conflict, the majority of them civilians. The use of the bomb thus took place in a world that had grown used to killing on a scale unimaginable in earlier times.

In the course of the Second World War, the air forces of Britain and the United States carried out a devastating bombing campaign against targets in Germany. This picture shows the ruins of Dresden, a city struck by air raids in February 1945 in which many tens of thousands of civilians were killed.

The origins of the war lay in the ambitions of aggressive militarist governments that came to power in Germany and Japan in the 1930s. In September 1939 Germany, ruled by Nazi dictator Adolf Hitler, invaded Poland. Britain and France, the leading democratic countries in Europe, responded by declaring war on Germany. The Germans defeated France in June 1940 and invaded the Soviet Union in the following summer.

Meanwhile, the Japanese had set out to create an empire in Asia. Officially under the rule of Emperor Hirohito, in the 1930s Japan was dominated by army and navy officers. They launched an invasion of China in 1937 and in 1940 moved troops into parts of south-east Asia. American president Franklin D. Roosevelt tried to use America's economic power to stop Japanese expansion. In the summer of 1941 the United States organized a complete block on the supply of oil to Japan. The Japanese army was totally dependent on imported oil to continue its operations. Japan's leaders faced a choice between abandoning their ambitions to build an Asian empire or going to war with the United States. They chose war.

America Enters the War

The Japanese attacked the American naval base at Pearl Harbor on 7 December 1941. Three days later Germany declared war on the United States. The Americans thus found themselves involved in two theatres of war. In Europe and North Africa the United States fought against Germany and its associates. America's main allies in the European theatre were Britain and the Soviet Union. In the Pacific and south-east Asia, the United States and Britain fought the Japanese. The Soviet Union did not join in the war against Japan until the very end. In 1943 the Allies declared a policy of 'unconditional surrender'. This meant there could be no peace negotiations to end the war. Germany and Japan would have to accept defeat and allow the Allies to occupy their country and do what they wanted with it.

The British and Americans saw themselves as fighting for freedom against slavery. They regarded the regimes ruling Germany and Japan as evil and barbaric. They felt justified in using almost any means to win the war, including bombing enemy cities. Before they entered the war, America's leaders were outspokenly critical of what Roosevelt called 'the ruthless bombing from the air of civilians'. But after the United States entered the war, American bombers joined with the RAF in devastating raids on German cities. The United States

The scene of mayhem at the American Pearl Harbor base during the Japanese surprise attack on 7 December 1941. The American aircraft are still on the ground, having failed to take off in time to counter the Japanese onslaught.

TURNING POINT

Pearl Harbor

In the first week of December 1941 a Japanese fleet, including six aircraft carriers, sailed undetected to within flying range of the American Pacific naval base at Pearl Harbor, Hawaii. America's leaders knew that a war with Japan was likely to begin any day, but personnel at Pearl Harbor were not alert to the threat. On 7 December Japanese naval aircraft attacked the base, achieving total surprise. Eighteen US ships were sunk, including four battleships, although crucially none of America's aircraft carriers was in port and so all survived. Around 3,500 American servicemen were killed. This 'sneak attack', without a formal declaration of war, shocked and outraged the American people. Americans often referred to Pearl Harbor as a justification for showing no mercy to the Japanese.

always claimed to be attacking military targets – including factories producing war equipment – but inevitably many thousands of civilians were killed in the raids. On the whole, ordinary people in Britain and America welcomed the bombing of German cities, especially as the Germans themselves had bombed London and other European cities.

The Americans felt even less inhibition about bombing cities in Japan, because in the Second World War they hated the Japanese much more than they hated the Germans or any other of their enemies. From February 1942, some 110,000 people of Japanese origin, many of them full American citizens, were forcibly removed from the west coast of the United States and herded into camps. No such action was taken against Americans of German origin. Of course, Germany had not directly attacked the United States, but there was unquestionably an element of racism in the American attitude to the Japanese. In an opinion poll conducted in the United States in December

Members of a Japanese-American family in California await transfer to an internment camp in the United States in 1942. Most white Americans felt that the Japanese were an alien race who could not be trusted even when they had taken American citizenship.

VOICES FROM THE PAST
Not human beings

In an article about the fighting on the Pacific island of Guadalcanal in 1942, American journalist John Hersey described the attitude of US Marines towards the Japanese:

'Quite frequently you hear Marines say: "I wish we were fighting against the Germans. They are human beings like us… But the Japs are like animals… They take to the jungle as if they had been bred there, and like some beasts you never see them until they are dead."'

Quoted in Richard Rhodes, *The Making of the Atomic Bomb* (Penguin, 1986)

Territory controlled by the Japanese, 1942

By mid-1942 the Japanese armed forces had control of a vast area stretching from the islands of the central Pacific to Burma and from Manchuria to the Netherlands East Indies (Indonesia). The Japanese claimed to be liberating Asian people from rule by white people, and called the area under their control the 'Greater East Asia Prosperity Sphere'. However, they behaved as brutally to fellow Asians as they did to Allied prisoners of war.

1944, one in three people said they thought Japan should cease to exist as a country when the war ended, and one in eight said that the entire Japanese population should be exterminated.

Japanese Atrocities

After Pearl Harbor, regarded by the American public as a totally unprovoked attack, hatred of the Japanese had been increased by accounts of their brutal mistreatment of Allied prisoners. In the first stage of the Pacific war, the Japanese army swiftly conquered Singapore and the Philippines and advanced as far as Indonesia and Burma. Allied soldiers captured during this period of Japanese triumph were often starved, beaten, tortured or executed. About one in four Allied prisoners of the Japanese died in captivity. The Japanese were equally brutal towards fellow Asians, massacring large numbers of Chinese and of Filipinos.

The fighting in the Pacific War was merciless. From 1943 onwards, the Americans drove the Japanese back across the Pacific island by island. As the fighting drew closer to Japan, casualties on both sides mounted steeply. The Japanese had been taught to die willingly for their emperor and their homeland. They mostly fought to the death rather than surrender. American soldiers were totally ruthless in return. They rarely took prisoners, mostly killing every

Emperor Hirohito (right) inspects an area of Tokyo devastated by American bombing in March 1945. Exhausted and bewildered survivors of the bombing failed to greet the emperor with the enthusiasm and devotion normally expected of them.

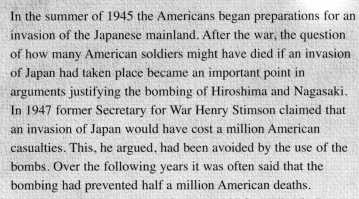

HOW DID IT HAPPEN?
Estimated death tolls

In the summer of 1945 the Americans began preparations for an invasion of the Japanese mainland. After the war, the question of how many American soldiers might have died if an invasion of Japan had taken place became an important point in arguments justifying the bombing of Hiroshima and Nagasaki. In 1947 former Secretary for War Henry Stimson claimed that an invasion of Japan would have cost a million American casualties. This, he argued, had been avoided by the use of the bombs. Over the following years it was often said that the bombing had prevented half a million American deaths.

However, historian Barton J. Bernstein found that in June 1945 US military planners estimated that an invasion of Japan the following November would cost 25,000 US lives, with a further 21,000 dying if a follow-up invasion was required in 1946. Another 170,000 Americans were expected to be wounded in the two invasions. Bernstein wrote: 'The myth of 500,000 American lives saved thus seems to have no basis in fact.' A number of historians have nonetheless continued to assert that much higher casualty estimates were being mentioned by some senior generals at the time.

Barton J. Bernstein quoted in Michael J. Hogan (ed.) *Hiroshima in History and Memory* (Cambridge University Press, 1996)

'Jap' they could find. From October 1944 Japanese airmen adopted desperate 'kamikaze' tactics, deliberately crashing their aircraft on to the decks of Allied warships. The suicidal courage of the Japanese convinced the Americans that Japan was unlikely to agree to surrender until it was utterly crushed.

By November 1944 the advancing American forces were able to establish air bases on Pacific islands within range of Japanese cities. The bombing did not have a major impact, however, until March 1945, when US aircraft began to carry out mass raids at night using firebombs – incendiaries.

These raids, ordered by Major-General Curtis LeMay, were devastatingly effective. Japanese buildings were mostly made of wood and paper. When 300 aircraft of US 20th Bomber Command attacked Tokyo on the night of 9–10 March they started a fire that destroyed 39 square kilometres of the city and may have killed as many as 100,000 people.

A Japanese fighter aircraft tries to crash onto the deck of an American warship, USS *Missouri*. Such 'kamikaze' suicide attacks showed the readiness of the Japanese to sacrifice their lives in the defence of their homeland and their emperor.

Civilian Deaths

American leaders were certainly aware that bombing civilians was a questionable way of waging war. There had been public protests in February 1945 when Allied bombers – mostly British – devastated the German city of Dresden, killing an estimated 60,000 people to no clear military purpose. So the United States continued officially to insist that its bombing of Japanese cities was aimed at military targets such as barracks, ports and factories.

During the spring and summer of 1945 air raids battered city after city across Japan. At the same time, the fiercest battle of the Pacific war took place on the island of Okinawa. During three months of fighting – from April through June – some 12,500 American soldiers were killed and 36,500 wounded. Japanese dead in the battle for Okinawa numbered around 220,000, made up of almost equal numbers of soldiers and civilians. But although Japan's soldiers were losing battle after battle and its cities were being reduced to ashes, there was little sign of a weakening of the Japanese people's will to fight. In summer 1945 it was widely expected that the war would continue into 1946. But, in secret, preparations were under way to hit Japan with a weapon of unprecedented power: the atomic bomb.

3 The Manhattan Project

The invention of the atom bomb was a result of progress in the science of physics in the early decades of the 20th century. In 1905, in his Theory of Relativity, German-born scientist Albert Einstein stated that even a small amount of matter could theoretically be transformed into a large amount of energy. By the 1930s physicists had begun to discover ways of releasing some of the energy held in the atoms of which all matter is composed. In experiments, uranium atoms were split. This process of 'fission' released energy from the atom's nucleus. Physicists realized that, in principle, it would be possible to set up a chain reaction in which large numbers of atoms were split in a very short time. The amount of energy released would be vast – in other words, there would be a massive explosion.

The theory behind what became known as an 'atom bomb' had been worked out by 1939 – the year in which the Second World War began in Europe. It was not a secret. All major countries involved in the war had scientists who knew that an atom bomb was theoretically possible. But no one knew if it would be possible in practice to make such a weapon, nor did they know how long such a project might take.

A considerable number of leading scientists were Jewish. Nazi dictator Adolf Hitler hated Jews. After Hitler came to power in 1933, discrimination and harassment by the Nazi regime forced Jewish scientists working in Germany to flee abroad, mostly to Britain or the United States. Einstein himself was driven out of Germany, going to live and work in America.

German-born scientist Albert Einstein and his daughter Margaret take the oath to become citizens of the United States in October 1940. Although he was the most famous scientist in the world, Einstein had been forced out of Nazi Germany because he was Jewish, and for that reason unacceptable to the racist Nazi government.

```
                                    Albert Einstein
                                    Old Grove Rd.
                                    Nassau Point
                                    Peconic, Long Island

                                    August 2nd, 1939

F.D. Roosevelt,
President of the United States,
White House
Washington, D.C.


Sir:

        Some recent work by E.Fermi and L. Szilard, which has been com-
municated to me in manuscript, leads me to expect that the element uran-
ium may be turned into a new and important source of energy in the im-
mediate future. Certain aspects of the situation which has arisen seem
to call for watchfulness and, if necessary, quick action on the part
of the Administration. I believe therefore that it is my duty to bring
to your attention the following facts and recommendations:

        In the course of the last four months it has been made probable -
through the work of Joliot in France as well as Fermi and Szilard in
America - that it may become possible to set up a nuclear chain reaction
in a large mass of uranium,by which vast amounts of power and large quant-
ities of new radium-like elements would be generated. Now it appears
almost certain that this could be achieved in the immediate future.

        This new phenomenon would also lead to the construction of bombs,
and it is conceivable - though much less certain - that extremely power-
ful bombs of a new type may thus be constructed. A single bomb of this
type, carried by boat and exploded in a port, might very well destroy
the whole port together with some of the surrounding territory. However,
such bombs might very well prove to be too heavy for transportation by
air.
```

This is the first page of the letter written by Albert Einstein to President Roosevelt, alerting him to the possibility of an atomic bomb. Although written in August 1939, the letter was not delivered to Roosevelt until October, by which time war had broken out in Europe.

Hitler and the Bomb

When war broke out, scientists of Jewish origin were especially worried that, if Germany was first to make an atom bomb, their sworn enemy Hitler might use it to achieve world domination. As one of them, Rudolph Peierls, said: 'The thought of Hitler being in possession of such a weapon with nobody else being able to hit back was of course very frightening…' They felt it was vital that Britain or the United States should beat Germany in the race to build the bomb. Einstein wrote to President Roosevelt explaining that 'extremely powerful bombs of a new type' could be built. After receiving the letter in October 1939, Roosevelt responded by setting up a 'uranium committee' to promote atom bomb research.

At first, however, it was scientists working in Britain who made the most progress. By the time the United States entered the war in December 1941, these scientists had already discovered how a controlled atomic explosion could be created. Their work was top

The person in overall charge of the Manhattan Project was US army officer General Leslie Groves (right). He is seen here with nuclear physicist Robert Oppenheimer, who was director of the scientific research at Los Alamos, New Mexico.

secret, but once the United States became an ally, the knowledge was passed on to the Americans. The British realized that they did not have the enormous resources that would be needed to build an atom bomb; the United States did.

The American atom bomb programme, launched in December 1941, was codenamed the Manhattan Project. An army officer, General Leslie R. Groves, was put in charge, aided by American physicist Robert Oppenheimer as scientific director. Roosevelt gave the project an unlimited budget. In effect, Groves was told he and his team could have any resources they needed. Groves later described his mission as 'to get this thing done and used as fast as possible'.

An international team of nuclear scientists was assembled, many transferred from the British bomb project. They worked in several locations, including Chicago, where America's first nuclear reactor was built in 1942. But the main site for scientific research was at Los Alamos in the wilds of New Mexico. Here some 6,000 people were eventually housed – mostly scientists, technicians and their families – largely cut off from contact with the outside world.

The Manhattan Project involved much more than just scientific research and experiment, however. It was also a vast engineering and industrial programme, which at its peak employed around 200,000 people across the United States. Most of them had no idea what they were working on. Despite the scale of the project, it was kept a secret from the public and even from most American political and military leaders. The massive sum spent on the project – $2 billion in total – was hidden from the US Congress, because Congressmen were not allowed to know the project existed.

Approaching Readiness

One by one, the daunting scientific and technical problems were overcome. By the summer of 1944 Groves was able to report to Roosevelt that the first atom bombs would be ready for use in the

VOICES FROM THE PAST

Race to beat the Germans

Otto Frisch, one of the scientists who worked on the Manhattan Project, explained what motivated him and his colleagues:

'Why start on a project which, if successful, would end with the production of a weapon of unparalleled violence, a weapon of mass destruction such as the world had never seen? The answer was very simple. We were at war and … very probably some German scientists had had the same idea and were working on it.'

Quoted in Richard Rhodes, *The Making of the Atomic Bomb* (Penguin, 1986)

An atomic device is raised to a platform on a tower at Alamogordo in the New Mexican desert, in preparation for the world's first atomic test in July 1945. The test explosion was the culmination of two years' intensive work on bomb design and assembly by the nuclear scientists at Los Alamos, New Mexico, that formed part of the Manhattan Project.

following year. Groves set about organizing a special bomber group that would be ready to drop the bombs as soon as they were built.

By that time the Germans had long abandoned their atom bomb project. They had decided it was not a realistic proposition – which, given the resources they had available, was probably true for them. The threat of a Nazi bomb, which had been the original motive for setting up the Manhattan Project, had ceased to exist. Indeed, by the end of 1944 both Germany and Japan were facing certain defeat.

Yet the American atom bomb project continued at full speed. Many people involved in the project, including Groves himself, were determined to produce the bomb in time for it to be used against the enemy. They felt that if the war was over before the bomb was built, all their efforts would be wasted – and it would be hard to justify the immense sums of money that had been spent on the project without the approval of Congress. The bomb was now regarded (by the small number of people who knew of its existence) as a weapon that might possibly end the war at a stroke, by forcing the enemy to surrender.

German General Alfred Jodl signs the unconditional surrender document at Rheims, France, on 7 May 1945, ending the war in Europe. The defeat of Germany allowed the Allies to focus all their efforts on the continuing war against Japan.

When it became clear that Nazi Germany was not capable of building an atom bomb and was losing the war, a number of scientists involved in the Manhattan Project began to question what they were doing. One of their major concerns was that the atom bomb was being kept a secret, instead of being shared with America's wartime ally the

Soviet Union. A few scientists even acted as Soviet spies, passing information on the project to the Soviet Union. But the majority of scientists on the project expressed no special concern about plans to use the bomb against Japan or relations with the Soviets.

The Interim Committee

In May 1945 Germany surrendered. This left Japan as the only possible target for the atom bomb. In the same month, an Interim Committee was set up to advise the president on matters relating to the bomb. The committee was chaired by US Secretary of War Henry L. Stimson and had a panel of scientific advisers that included Oppenheimer. In the course of its discussions the committee considered two alternatives to dropping the bomb on a Japanese city. One was to demonstrate the power of the bomb by dropping it in a deserted place. The other was to tell the Japanese when and on which city the bomb was going to be dropped, so they could move the population to safety. Neither of these options seemed practical to the committee and its members agreed unanimously that the bomb should be used without warning against Japan.

Henry Stimson, the US Secretary of War, had once been an outspoken critic of the bombing of civilians. He approved the use of the atom bomb, however, arguing that it saved lives by shortening the war.

TURNING POINT

The Franck Report

In May-June 1945 a number of Manhattan Project scientists based in Chicago decided to write to the US Secretary of State for War, Henry Stimson, expressing their concerns about the atom bomb. This document is known as the Franck Report after one of the scientists involved, James Franck.

The Franck Report pointed out how massively destructive any future global conflict fought with atomic weapons would be. The report suggested that a first step towards a general agreement to renounce the use of atomic weapons in the future would be for the Americans to renounce using the atom bomb against Japan. If America did drop the bomb on a Japanese city, other countries might lose confidence in the United States with 'a wave of horror and repulsion sweeping over the rest of the world...'

American political and military leaders ignored the opinions of the Chicago scientists.

VOICES FROM THE PAST

Destroyer of worlds

Robert Oppenheimer, the scientific director of the Manhattan Project, was one of those who witnessed the first atomic test at Alamogordo. He later wrote:

'We waited until the blast had passed, walked out of the shelter, and then it was extremely solemn. We knew the world would not be the same. A few people laughed, a few people cried. Most people were silent. I remembered the line from the Hindu scripture, the Baghavad-gita: ... "Now I am become death, the destroyer of worlds." I suppose we all thought that, one way or another.'

Quoted in Len Giovanetti and Fred Freed, *The Decision to Drop the Bomb* (Methuen, 1967)

This is an atom bomb of the same kind as 'Little Boy' dropped on Hiroshima. Key components for Little Boy were carried to Tinian Island in July 1945 on board USS *Indianapolis* – a ship that was sunk by a Japanese submarine only three days after making the delivery.

Another committee, the Target Committee chaired by Groves, had the job of deciding on suitable targets for atomic attack. The committee was supposed to choose a military target, but since most of Japan's population were in some way or another contributing to the war effort, the idea of a 'military target' could include almost every town or city in the country. The committee wanted the target to be big enough to show the full effect of the bomb, so they focused on cities that were larger than the area the bomb was expected to destroy. Also to show the bomb's power to the full, they needed to find cities that had not already been reduced to rubble and ashes by US aircraft.

Hiroshima was chosen as an ideal target. It had a port and an army base, justifying it as a military target. It was large enough and mostly undamaged. And it was flat, which would give the bomb maximum effect. Deciding on other targets was less easy. Nagasaki was only added to the list late on – although it was the site of important factories, it was too hilly for the bomb to have its full effect.

The US air forces were ordered not to attack the chosen cities while the Manhattan Project team made their final preparations. Two types of bomb were built. One, using uranium, was nicknamed Little Boy. Its technology was considered totally reliable, so it did not need to be tested. The other bomb, using plutonium, was called Fat Man. Scientists at Los Alamos were less sure that Fat Man would work, so they organized a test explosion of a plutonium device.

The test took place just before dawn on 16 July 1945 at Alamogordo in the New Mexico desert. The explosion was even more powerful than expected – equivalent to over 18,000 tonnes of TNT. It produced a flash of light brighter than any previously seen on Earth and temperatures three times hotter than the core of the Sun. As they watched the mushroom cloud rise to over 12,000 metres above their heads, the scientists and technicians who had gathered to witness the test were delighted at its success. But they were also chilled by a realization of the awesome power they had unleashed upon the world.

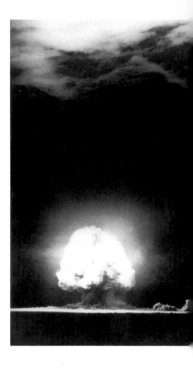

The world's first atomic explosion takes place at Alamogordo, New Mexico, on 16 July 1945. Observers more than 10 km away from the explosion recorded feeling a wave of heat on their faces as if someone had opened the door of a hot oven.

HOW DID IT HAPPEN?
Demonstrating the bomb

The Franck Report (see page 21) suggested dropping the bomb on 'a desert or barren island' to demonstrate its power to the Japanese and avoid the need to drop it on a city. Admiral Lewis Strauss, a member of the Interim Committee, felt the bomb should be dropped on 'a large forest … not far from Tokyo.' But Robert Oppenheimer, on the Interim Committee's Scientific Panel, stated that no demonstration 'was likely to induce surrender'. Oppenheimer later commented that he doubted the Japanese would have been influenced by 'an enormous nuclear firecracker detonated at great height and doing little damage'.

The idea of a demonstration of the bomb was never taken seriously by the US government. Secretary of State James Byrnes also rejected the idea of warning the Japanese when and where the bomb would be used. He later wrote: 'We feared that, if the Japanese were told that the bomb would be used on a given locality, they might bring our boys who were prisoners of war to that area.' He also said that if the bomb had failed to work after the US had announced it was to be used, this would have 'given aid and comfort to the Japanese militarists.'

Strauss quoted in Gar Alperovitz, *Atomic Diplomacy* (Pluto Press 1994 edition); Oppenheimer quoted in Richard Rhodes, *The Making of the Atomic Bomb* (Penguin, 1986); Byrnes quoted in Len Giovanetti and Fred Freed, *The Decision to Drop the Bomb* (Methuen, 1967)

4 The Decision to Drop the Bomb

The summer of 1945 the United States had a new, inexperienced president – Harry S. Truman. Previously vice-president, he became president when Roosevelt died on 12 April. Such was the secrecy surrounding the Manhattan Project that Truman had not known of its existence until he assumed the presidency.

After the defeat of Germany in early May, Truman and his advisers were preoccupied with two crucial issues. One was how to defeat Japan as quickly as possible. The other was America's future relationship with its wartime ally, the Soviet Union. Soviet dictator Joseph Stalin had played a leading role in the Allied victory over Germany, but by the summer of 1945 relations between the Soviets and the Americans were already turning sour. There was particular disagreement over Poland, where the Soviet Union was bent on imposing Communist rule against the wishes of a large part of the population.

A convoy of Soviet army trucks drives through the ruins of Berlin after the fall of the city in May 1945. Relations between the Soviet Union and its wartime allies, the United States and Britain, worsened soon after the defeat of Germany.

The Potsdam Conference

In July 1945 Truman, Stalin and Churchill met for a conference at Potsdam, on the outskirts of Berlin, Germany. They were to discuss how Europe was to be organized in the postwar period and how the war with Japan was to be finished off. Truman and his secretary of state, James F. Byrnes, were acutely aware that their new secret weapon – the atom bomb – might give them a lot more bargaining power when talking to Stalin. They were delighted when, at the start of the Potsdam conference, news came through of the successful test at Alamogordo.

One of the Americans' declared motives in attending the Potsdam conference was to get Stalin to turn his military might against Japan. The Soviet Union had remained neutral with regard to the Pacific War, while fighting Germany. The Soviet Union had promised to declare war on Japan once the Germans were defeated. Now the Americans wanted them to live up to that promise.

But in private Truman and Byrnes had begun to wonder whether it might be better to keep the Soviets out of the war in the Far East. With the atom bomb almost ready, perhaps the United States could make Japan surrender quickly without the aid of Stalin. After all, if the Soviets helped defeat the Japanese, they would undoubtedly take the opportunity to extend

The leaders of the three major Allied powers meet at the opening of the Potsdam conference in July 1945: left to right, British prime minister Winston Churchill, American president Harry Truman, and Soviet dictator Joseph Stalin. Churchill lost a general election while the conference was in progress and Clement Attlee replaced him as prime minister of Great Britain.

TURNING POINT
Telling Stalin about the bomb

At the Potsdam Conference, the Americans and British hoped that the revelation of their new secret weapon would come as a great shock to Stalin. On 24 July, behaving with deliberate casualness, Truman mentioned to the Soviet leader that the United States possessed a new weapon 'of unusual destructive force'. Stalin's response was disappointingly cool. He calmly welcomed the news and hoped that they would make 'good use' of the weapon against the Japanese. In fact, Stalin already knew about the bomb through spies at Los Alamos and elsewhere, although he probably did not appreciate its full significance until the destruction of Hiroshima.

US Marines engage in the tough fighting for possession of the Japanese island of Okinawa in May 1945. The heavy losses suffered in taking Okinawa made American leaders fear that invading the Japanese mainland would cost tens of thousands of soldiers' lives.

their power and influence in the Far East. Truman was clearly in two minds on this issue. On 18 July, when Stalin agreed to go to war with Japan the following month, the president wrote to his wife: 'I've gotten what I came for.' Yet in conversations with Byrnes he expressed hopes that the bomb might make the Japanese surrender before the Soviets entered the conflict.

Meanwhile, although publicly Japan maintained an attitude of national unity and total defiance, the Japanese government was split in its attitude to continuing the war. Convinced that Japan's position was hopeless, some leading figures such as Foreign Minister Shigenori Togo wanted to negotiate an immediate end to the fighting. But others, including Minister of War General Korechika Anami, were determined that Japan should fight to the finish. From June 1945 onwards, those in favour of negotiation had the tentative backing of Emperor Hirohito.

The Possibility of Peace

Allied leaders knew a lot about the conflicting attitudes of the Japanese government. American spies had cracked Japanese codes and were able to read secret messages such as those sent from Japan to its embassies in foreign cities. As a result, they were aware that the emperor had given his support to the idea of using the neutral Soviet Union as go-between in peace negotiations with the Allies. But they were also aware that even those Japanese leaders in favour of peace negotiations still wanted to avoid actual surrender. In one intercepted message sent to the Japanese ambassador in Moscow in July, Togo said: 'It is His Majesty's heart's desire to see the swift termination of the war... However, as long as England and America insist on unconditional surrender our country has no alternative but ... an all-out effort for the sake of survival and the honour of the homeland.' The Allies, for their part, had no intention of negotiating with the Japanese. For them, nothing short of total surrender would do.

Emperor Hirohito opens a sitting of the Japanese parliament in 1945. In practice the Japanese parliament wielded no real power; all decisions were taken by a Supreme War Leadership Council.

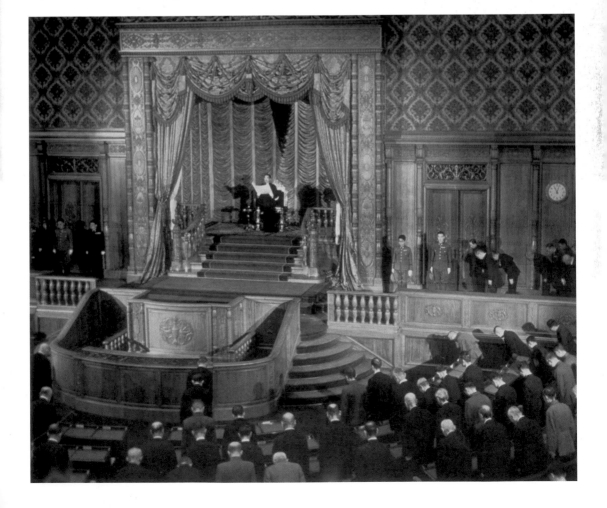

From March 1945 until the end of the war the following August, American bombing raids devastated Japanese cities. Attacking by night, hundreds of B-29 bombers dropped incendiary bombs that started huge firestorms in cities where most of the buildings were made of wood.

A military strategy for defeating Japan had been hammered out by Allied military and political leaders in the summer of 1945. The heads of the US army, navy and air force had each argued that their own service could win the war. The navy said that a blockade of Japanese ports would force Japan to surrender because its population would starve for lack of imported food and its industries would collapse without imported raw materials. The air force argued that its bombing raids would soon lay waste to every Japanese city and leave Japan no choice but to give in. Army commanders were in favour of an invasion of Japan, arguing that only the occupation of at least part of the country by Allied troops would finally break the Japanese will to resist.

Instead of choosing between these approaches, Truman in effect planned to proceed with all of them at once. The navy would blockade Japan; the air force would bomb the cities; and the army would mount an invasion of Kyushu, southern Japan, in November 1945. There were also plans for a follow-up invasion of central Japan in March 1946, if necessary. US military planners estimated that the invasion of Kyushu would probably cost the lives of around 25,000 American

VOICES FROM THE PAST
'That awful thing'

General Dwight D. Eisenhower later described his reaction when told by Secretary for War Stimson about the decision to use the atom bomb against Japan:

'I was getting more and more depressed just thinking about it. Then he asked for my opinion, so I told him I was against it on two counts. First, the Japanese were ready to surrender and it wasn't necessary to hit them with that awful thing. Second, I hated to see our country be the first to use such as weapon.'

Quoted in Richard Rhodes, *The Making of the Atomic Bomb* (Penguin, 1986)

In June 1945 General Dwight D. Eisenhower was an American hero for leading the campaign that defeated Germany. He had no power, however, over the decision to drop the atom bomb – a decision he regretted.

servicemen. If the second invasion was needed, the planners estimated a further 21,000 Americans would die.

When these various options were discussed, no mention was made of the atom bomb. Many senior American military commanders did not know of its existence until they were told at Potsdam the following month. Those who did know of the bomb were very sceptical about 'secret weapons'. They doubted that the bomb would work or believed that it would be much less powerful than was predicted.

Some military commanders were opposed to the use of the bomb on principle. Both Admiral William D. Leahy, the US Chief of Staff, and General Dwight D. Eisenhower, the Supreme Commander of Allied Forces in Europe, expressed their moral doubts in private. But there was never a formal meeting of American military and political leaders to discuss whether or not the bomb should be used.

Bombs Reach Tinian

While the Potsdam conference was going on, Groves went ahead with preparations to drop the bomb as quickly as possible. The materials for the first bomb were shipped to Tinian island, where Tibbets' B-29s

were already stationed. Groves informed Truman that the first bomb (Little Boy) would be assembled and ready to drop by early August. The second (Fat Man) would be ready shortly afterwards, with a third bomb following later in the month. On 25 July Truman formally authorized the use of atom bombs against Japan.

The following day, at the end of the Potsdam conference, the Allies issued a statement calling on the Japanese to surrender. This is known as the Potsdam Declaration. It tried to reassure the Japanese that the Allies did not intend to exterminate them or subject them to permanent foreign

The Fat Man atomic bomb – later dropped on Nagasaki – was assembled and readied for use on Tinian island. Ground crew scrawled various messages to the Japanese on the tail fin.

rule, but was otherwise uncompromising. In an early draft of the declaration, it said that the Allies might allow the Japanese emperor to stay on the throne, but this was cut out of the final version. The declaration ended: 'We call upon the government of Japan to proclaim now the unconditional surrender of all Japanese armed forces... The alternative for Japan is prompt and utter destruction.'

VOICES FROM THE PAST

Truman's diary

During the Potsdam conference, Truman kept a diary. It reveals his discomfort with the idea that the atom bomb was going to be used against civilians. Despite knowing the bomb was to be dropped on the city of Hiroshima, on 25 July Truman wrote:

'...military objectives and soldiers and sailors are the target and not women and children. Even if the Japs are savages, ruthless, merciless and fanatic, we as the leader of the world for the common welfare [are not]. The target will be a purely military one.'

Quoted in Michael J. Hogan (ed.) *Hiroshima in History and Memory* (Cambridge University Press, 1996)

HOW DID IT HAPPEN?

Reasons for using the bomb

On 9 August 1945 President Truman told the American people why the atom bomb had been used against Japan: 'We have used it in order to shorten the agony of war, in order to save the lives of thousands and thousands of young Americans.'

In the 1960s, however, historian Gar Alperovitz controversially argued that the main reason the bombs were dropped was not to end the war, but to intimidate the Soviet Union. Martin J. Sherwin supported this view in *A World Destroyed*. Sherwin argued that Truman deliberately stuck to demanding unconditional surrender – which he knew the Japanese would reject – because 'he preferred to use the atomic bomb' to demonstrate its power to the Soviets.

Today the majority of historians agree that US leaders were aware of the impact dropping the bomb would have on relations with the Soviet Union. But most believe that the bomb was primarily used in the straightforward hope of hastening the defeat of Japan by hitting them as hard as possible. In the words of historian J. Samuel Walker: 'US officials always assumed that the bomb would be used and saw no reason not to use it once it became available.'

Truman and Walker quoted in Michael J. Hogan (ed.) *Hiroshima in History and Memory* (Cambridge University Press, 1996); Martin J. Sherwin, *A World Destroyed* (Knopf, 1975)

The Potsdam Declaration has since been criticized on two counts. Some people have argued that if the Americans had said that the Japanese emperor would be allowed to remain on the throne, Japan might have surrendered. It has also been argued that the Japanese should have been given a more precise warning of the new weapon that was about to hit them – the reference to 'prompt and utter destruction' was simply too vague and obscure.

As it was, Japanese Prime Minister Kantaro Suzuki rejected the Potsdam Declaration contemptuously on 28 July, calling it a 'rehash' of previous calls for unconditional surrender and saying he intended to 'ignore it'. From that point onwards the dropping of the atom bomb on Hiroshima was inevitable.

Stalin (in white) attends one of the round-table meetings at the Potsdam conference. The Americans hoped that their possession of the atom bomb would force the Soviet dictator to compromise on issues such as the future of Poland.

5 The Surrender Decision

By August 1945 the Japanese were staring defeat in the face. Almost of all of their shipping – both merchant vessels and warships – had been sunk and their cities were defenceless against American air attack. Since the surrender of Nazi Germany, Japan did not have a single friend or ally in the world. On the other hand, Japanese forces still remained in control of Korea, much of China and south-east Asia. And the Japanese people were preparing for a last-ditch defence of their homeland.

Despite his secret leanings towards peace negotiations, Emperor Hirohito had publicly ordered the entire nation to prepare for total resistance to the enemy which would 'achieve the goals of the war'. Japanese military leaders planned to resist an Allied invasion with extensive use of suicide tactics, not only in the air but on sea and land. The government-controlled newspapers continued to urge the Japanese people to be ready to die for their emperor.

The dropping of the atom bomb on Hiroshima on 6 August at first caused only confusion among Japan's political and military leaders. They were

Japanese children stand among the ruins of Hiroshima. They are wearing face masks as protection against the smell of thousands of rotting corpses.

VOICES FROM THE PAST

Millions facing death

Koichi Kido, the Japanese emperor's chief adviser, later described the desperate state of his country in summer 1945:

'The cities of Japan were being burned by bombings…At least one city and at times two were being turned into ashes daily…The food situation was becoming worse and worse. Under such conditions even the soldiers had not much to eat. There was nothing in Japan… With winter ahead …tens of millions of people [faced] dying a dog's death from hunger and exposure.'

Quoted in Len Giovanetti and Fred Freed, *The Decision to Drop the Bomb* (Methuen, 1967)

not sure about what type of bomb it had been or the true extent of the destruction caused. All lines of communication between the Japanese capital, Tokyo, and Hiroshima had been cut by the effect of the immense explosion. It was not until the morning of 8 August that Japan's leaders learned for sure that an entire city had been destroyed by a single bomb.

On that same day, the Soviet Union declared war on Japan. Over a million Soviet troops were massed along the border between the Soviet Union and Japanese-occupied Manchuria. At one o'clock on the morning of 9 August the Soviets attacked, soon advancing into Manchurian territory.

Double Blow

The double blow of the destruction of Hiroshima and the Soviet attack at last convinced the Japanese political and military leaders that an urgent attempt must be made to end the war as speedily as possible. At 11 a.m. on 9 August the Japanese Supreme War Council met in Tokyo to consider on what terms they might be prepared to surrender. Foreign Minister Togo argued that Japan should surrender on only one condition: that the emperor remain on his throne. The majority of the council still wanted to insist on other conditions, including that Japan should not be occupied by Allied troops.

Japanese troops in Manchuria practise rifle shooting just before the Soviet invasion of 9 August 1945. The Japanese defences proved completely inadequate and were swept aside by the Soviet onslaught.

As the War Council met to discuss these issues, a second atom bomb was dropped, this time on the city of Nagasaki. The haste with which the second bomb was dropped has often been criticized, since the Japanese government had not been given adequate time to respond to the Hiroshima bombing. However, General Groves's instructions were to continue dropping atom bombs on Japan until the Japanese surrendered or until he received an order from the president to stop. The second bombing had originally been scheduled for 11 August, but weather forecasts suggested that by then the weather over Japan might be too bad. As a result, preparations had been speeded up ready for a raid on 9 August.

By then the weather had in fact already worsened. The B-29 carrying the second bomb, piloted by Major Charles W. Sweeney, encountered storms on its way from Tinian to Japan. Sweeney's orders were to drop the bomb on the city of Kokura, but when he

A mushroom cloud rises over Nagasaki after the dropping of the Fat Man atomic bomb on the city on 9 August 1945. The bomb was dropped from a B-29 nicknamed Bock's Car, piloted by Major Charles Sweeney.

arrived over the target it was hidden by cloud cover. After circling for a while in hope of a break in the clouds, Sweeney headed for his secondary target, the port city of Nagasaki. This was also under heavy cloud. As he was running short of fuel, Sweeney decided to drop the bomb anyway, in the general direction of the invisible aiming point.

Nagasaki Bombing

The bomb, codenamed Fat Man, was a plutonium device of the kind tested at Alamogordo. It exploded at 11.02 a.m., about 2.5 km from its aiming point. Estimates of the death toll in Nagasaki vary from 35,000 to 80,000. That fewer people were killed than in the Hiroshima bombing was largely because of geography. Nagasaki was built on hills and valleys. The valley over which the bomb exploded was utterly devastated, but the hills around the valley sheltered other parts of the city from the full effect of the blast and radiation.

Despite the news of the bombing of Nagasaki, Japanese leaders in Tokyo remained deadlocked over surrender terms throughout 9 August. The Minister for War Korechika Anami and the army and navy chiefs of staff continued to insist that the country could fight on if necessary. Finally the emperor was called upon to resolve the deadlock. At 2 a.m. on the morning of 10 August, at a meeting held in an underground bomb shelter at the imperial palace, Hirohito declared himself in favour of immediate surrender because if not 'the Japanese race would perish'. The Japanese then told the Allies that they were ready to surrender as long as 'the prerogatives of His Majesty as a Sovereign Ruler' were not affected. In other words, Hirohito must remain on the throne.

The scale of the destruction at Nagasaki, although less total than at Hiroshima, was still awesome. In the valley that took the full force of the bomb blast, only a few concrete buildings were left standing.

Surrender Terms

Truman was not prepared to openly accept this condition. He knew that most of the American public regarded Hirohito in the same light as Hitler. An opinion poll had shown that one in three Americans wanted the emperor hanged as a war criminal. So a cautious reply was formulated that tried to leave the issue of Hirohito's future open. It stated that, after surrender, the emperor would come under the authority of the Allied supreme commander and that eventually the Japanese people would be free to choose their own form of

TURNING POINT
The emperor's broadcast

On the night of 14–15 August 1945 Emperor Hirohito recorded a radio broadcast to tell the Japanese people of the decision to surrender. It was the first time he had ever spoken to his people. In the speech he accepted that '…the war situation has developed not necessarily to Japan's advantage…' and referred to the 'cruel bomb' capable of causing 'incalculable' damage which had made it necessary to 'endure the unendurable'. Some army officers attempted to seize the recording to stop it being transmitted, but they failed. At noon on 15 August the speech was broadcast. Ordinary people were astonished to hear the sacred emperor talk in person. They found his ornate way of speaking very hard to understand. As they realized what he was saying, there was a sense of shock and many were in tears. Hiroshima doctor Hachiya recorded in his diary that for him the surrender 'produced a greater shock than the bombing of our city.'

US General Douglas MacArthur (in profile, far right) prepares to accept the Japanese delegation offering the formal surrender of Japan on board the battleship USS *Missouri* on 2 September 1945. This took place more than two weeks after Emperor Hirohito had announced the decision to surrender, effectively ending the war.

government. This reply once more split the Japanese leadership between those who wanted to accept the terms and those who did not.

Meanwhile, Truman had decided against using a third atom bomb, which was ready for shipping to Tinian island. The president reportedly stated that 'the thought of wiping out another 100,000 people was too horrible'. Conventional air attacks on Japan continued, however, with some of the heaviest raids of the war.

The Japanese people had been told nothing of the surrender negotiations and most were still fully committed to continuing the war. This was even true in Hiroshima. According to the diary of Hiroshima doctor Michihiko Hachiya, on 11 August a rumour spread around a hospital housing victims of the bombing; the rumour stated that Japan had retaliated with atom bomb attacks on American cities. Immediately 'everyone became cheerful and bright' and some of the victims 'began singing the victory song'.

Emperor Hirohito had no such illusions. On 14 August he informed Japanese political and military leaders that the country must 'bear the unbearable' and accept the Allied terms. Even at this late stage, some army officers attempted to mount a military coup to prevent the surrender. But loyalty to the emperor among senior officers was too strong and the coup attempt failed. At noon on 15 August Hirohito broadcast his radio message telling the Japanese people that the war was over.

Japanese prisoners of war on the island of Guam stand with heads bowed after the emperor's broadcast announcing Japan's surrender, 15 August 1945. Many Japanese people were profoundly shocked by the decision to surrender and only accepted it because of their loyalty to the emperor.

HOW DID IT HAPPEN?

Ending the war

It seemed obvious to most people in August 1945 that the atom bombs had ended the war, causing the Japanese surrender and avoiding the need for an invasion of Japan in November. However, the United States Strategic Bombing Survey, published shortly after the end of the war, stated that 'in all probability prior to 1 November 1945, Japan would have surrendered even if the atom bombs had not been dropped, even if Russia had not entered the war, and even if no invasion had been planned or contemplated'.

Over the last 60 years, most historians have agreed that Japan was already facing defeat at the time the bombs were dropped, but they have disagreed about how close Japan was to surrender. Barton J. Bernstein, for example, wrote that it was 'likely' that the war could have ended that summer without the atomic bombings, but 'far from definite'. Koichi Kido, Hirohito's chief adviser in summer 1945, believed that without the bomb it would have been difficult to get Japan's military leaders to accept the need for surrender. He said: 'The presence of the atomic bomb made it easier for us politicians to negotiate peace. Even then the military would not listen to reason.'

Bernstein quoted in Michael J. Hogan (ed.) *Hiroshima in History and Memory* (Cambridge University Press, 1996); Kido quoted in Len Giovanetti and Fred Freed, *The Decision to Drop the Bomb* (Methuen, 1967)

6 The Nuclear Age

At the end of August 1945, two weeks after the Japanese surrender, Allied soldiers began to arrive in Japan to occupy the country. They were able to witness the effect that the atom bombs had had on Hiroshima and Nagasaki. One American sailor, Osborn Elliot, later described the scene in Hiroshima, with 'women and children … sitting on the rubble that was once their homes' and many people wandering about 'with scars on their faces'.

Thousands of those affected by the bombing continued to die every day through late August and September. Most were victims of exposure to the nuclear radiation released by the bomb. The first symptom of this 'radiation sickness' was hair loss. This was followed by diarrhoea, fever and a chronic fall in the number of white blood cells in the body – an essential part of the body's defence against infection. The few doctors who had survived in the

A few American servicemen mingle with Japanese people shopping for goods salvaged from bombed-out buildings, Tokyo, October 1945. Despite the bitterness of the war, the American occupation of Japan went remarkably smoothly.

devastated cities were overwhelmed by the scale of the catastrophe and could do little to help the victims in their struggle to survive.

The Allied occupation forces, taking over what they regarded as a hostile country, imposed strict censorship on the Japanese media, preventing them from mentioning the effects of the bombing on Hiroshima and Nagasaki for three years after the war. The survivors received no special help from the authorities in coping with sickness, bereavement, disfigurement or psychological trauma. They were left to rebuild their lives as best they could.

By 1955, when this picture was taken, Hiroshima had already been extensively rebuilt. As Japan's economy boomed in the 1950s and 1960s, both Hiroshima and Nagasaki became thriving, bustling modern cities.

Japanese Recovery

Over time, Japan recovered from wartime devastation. In 1952 the country regained its independence, with a democratic system of government and Emperor Hirohito as its constitutional monarch. Instead of being enemies of the United States, the Japanese became the Americans' allies – the new enemy was the Soviet Union. Japan's economy also flourished in the 1950s and 1960s. Rapid industrial growth brought a new level of prosperity to the Japanese people. The cities of Hiroshima and Nagasaki shared in the economic boom. They were rebuilt and soon had larger populations than in 1945.

VOICES FROM THE PAST

Scarred by the bomb

A woman who survived the Hiroshima bomb described the fate of her daughter, suffering from radiation sickness, and her son, disfigured by the thick 'keloid' scars found on survivors:

'The sickness was so dreadful, but we could only look on helplessly. My daughter Nanako was so eager to live for the sake of her newborn baby, but she couldn't be saved... After Nanako died, I still had my 26-year-old son Hiromi; and he had keloid scars on his head and hands. Therefore, he couldn't get married, and he tried to commit suicide several times.'

Quoted in Kanzaburo Oe, *Hiroshima Notes* (Grove Press, 1996)

Seventeen-year-old Kunio Yamashita exhibits the raised 'keloid' scars that disfigured so many survivors of the Hiroshima and Nagasaki bombings. Fellow Japanese often shunned survivors, because they found their condition an embarrassing reminder of the past.

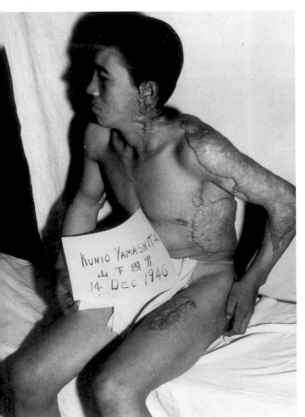

But the survivors of the bombings, known as hibakusha, continued to suffer, many scarred both in body and mind. The hibakusha were more likely than average to die from several forms of cancer, especially leukaemia. Over the years there were also many suicides that were blamed on the lingering mental impact of the bombing. On the other hand, fears that radiation damage might be handed down through the generations proved groundless. Although babies in the womb at the time of the bombing were harmed by radiation, children born to survivors in later years showed no signs of abnormality.

In the wider world, the bombing of Hiroshima and Nagasaki did not cause the 'wave of horror and repulsion' predicted in the Franck Report (see page 21). The savagery of the Second World War had blunted sensitivities to human suffering. The initial response in the Allied countries was predominantly one of relief that the war was ended, along with amazement at what Truman called 'the greatest achievement of organized science in history'. However, people could also immediately see that what had happened to Hiroshima and Nagasaki could at some point in the future be the fate of London and New York. A perilous new era had begun.

In the Soviet Union, Stalin's immediate reaction to the bombing of Hiroshima was to order his scientists and arms experts 'to provide us with atomic weapons in the shortest possible time'. With the help of information from spies in Britain and the United States, they achieved the task in four years. The first Soviet atom bomb test was carried out in September 1949.

By that time relations between the Soviet Union and its former wartime allies had already degenerated into a hostile confrontation that became known as the Cold War – 'cold' because it stopped short of direct armed conflict between the major powers. In the same year that the Soviet Union tested its first atom bomb, the United States formed the North Atlantic Treaty Organization (NATO), a military alliance with Britain and other West European countries designed to resist Soviet power. In 1955 the Soviet Union formed its own alliance, the Warsaw Pact, directed against NATO.

Truman signs the North Atlantic Treaty, founding the NATO alliance, on 29 August 1949. The treaty in effect meant that American nuclear weapons would be used to defend West European countries from any attack by the Soviet Union.

Nuclear Arms Race

Inevitably, given the hostility and mistrust between them, the two sides in the Cold War became involved in a nuclear arms race. The Americans and Soviets thus each sought to create bigger bombs and

The first hydrogen bomb test is carried out by the United States at Eniwetok Atoll in the Pacific on 6 November 1952. The small island of Elugelab, where the explosion took place, was completely vaporized.

more effective ways of delivering them to their targets. In 1952 the United States tested the first hydrogen bomb, a device using nuclear fusion rather than fission. The explosion was equivalent to over 10 million tonnes of TNT, making the bomb 500 times more powerful than the one that had destroyed Hiroshima. The Soviets soon produced their own hydrogen bomb and by the early 1960s were able to explode a device 1,000 times more powerful than the Hiroshima bomb. Britain, France and China also acquired nuclear weapons.

By the late 1950s missiles had been developed that could deliver nuclear warheads – essentially the same as hydrogen bombs – to targets thousands of kilometres distant. No city could be safe from potential destruction. Each side believed that the only effective way to defend itself against a devastating nuclear strike

TURNING POINT
The Cuban missile crisis

In 1959 Fidel Castro came to power in the Caribbean island of Cuba. He soon made his country an ally of the Soviet Union. In October 1962 the United States discovered that the Soviets were installing nuclear missiles in Cuba. US President John F. Kennedy ordered a naval blockade to stop Soviet ships carrying weapons to the island. For 13 days the two major nuclear powers stood on the brink of war. On 28 October, however, the Soviets agreed to dismantle their Cuban missile bases. The United States and the Soviet Union never came as close to nuclear war again.

VOICES FROM THE PAST

Against the bomb

Jonathan Schell, a prominent campaigner against nuclear weapons, wrote in 1982:

'There is no need to "abolish war" among the nuclear powers; it is already gone. The choices don't include war any longer. They consist now of peace, on the one hand, and annihilation on the other.'

Jonathan Schell, *The Fate of the Earth* (Jonathan Cape, 1982)

was to threaten the enemy with even worse destruction in return. Missiles and bomber aircraft were kept on 24-hour alert, ready to deliver an instant and overwhelmingly powerful response the moment an enemy attack was detected. The United States called this dangerous system for keeping the peace Mutually Assured Destruction – with the appropriate acronym MAD.

The closest the world came to a full-scale nuclear war was during the Cuban Missile Crisis in 1962. After this there were serious attempts to reduce the level of risk. The Americans and Soviets agreed to halt nuclear tests that had been releasing dangerous levels of radiation into the atmosphere. Between 1969 and 1979 talks between the two countries led to agreements to limit the number of nuclear weapons. However, the size of nuclear arsenals continued to grow. By the 1980s there were around 50,000 nuclear warheads in the world, each one many times bigger than the bomb dropped on Hiroshima.

Peace Protests

From the 1950s through to the 1980s, peace groups worldwide organized protests and demonstrations calling for nuclear disarmament. Some campaigners argued that a nuclear war would

British supporters of the Campaign for Nuclear Disarmament (CND) take part in a protest march to the nuclear research establishment at Aldermaston in 1961. Such protests attracted considerable support at a time when the threat of nuclear war seemed very real.

The remains of the former Hiroshima Industry Promotion Centre, partially destroyed by the atom bomb, have been preserved as a memorial in Hiroshima's Peace Park. The park is the site of demonstrations in favour of nuclear disarmament, held each year on the anniversary of the bombing.

be so destructive it could end life on Earth. The city of Hiroshima became an active participant in the peace movement. A Peace Museum and a Peace Park were opened in the city in 1955 and Hiroshima Day, 6 August, was commemorated there with an anti-nuclear protest each year.

An end to the nuclear arms race eventually came after Mikhail Gorbachev became leader of the Soviet Union in 1985. Gorbachev achieved a better relationship with the United States that ended the Cold War. His policies also unintentionally led to the break-up of the Soviet Union in 1991. Since that time negotiations between the United States and the new states which inherited Soviet nuclear weapons – chiefly Russia and Ukraine – have brought sharp reductions in numbers of warheads and missiles.

In the new millennium, six decades after the bombing of Hiroshima, a nuclear war between the major world powers seemed a very unlikely prospect. But this did not mean that the new risk introduced into the world by the invention of nuclear weapons had gone away. Despite efforts to prevent the spread of nuclear weapons, they had been acquired by more countries, including India, Pakistan and Israel. In the 2000s it was a major aim of US policy to prevent states such as Iran and North Korea – countries with governments the United States regarded as unreliable – from developing nuclear weapons. One of the main justifications given for the invasion of Iraq by American and British forces in 2003 was that Iraqi ruler Saddam Hussein was secretly pursuing a nuclear weapons programme. Perhaps even more worrying than states developing nuclear weapons was the possibility that a terrorist group might one day have the capacity to explode a nuclear device.

Yet it remained true that, 60 years into the nuclear age, the only nuclear weapons ever used were the bombs dropped on Hiroshima and Nagasaki. The Americans fought large-scale wars in Korea (1950-53) and Vietnam (1965-73) without resorting to their nuclear arsenal – although they nearly did so during the Korean War. India and Pakistan did not use them in their dispute over Kashmir, nor Israel in its confrontation with its Arab neighbours. Yet nothing proved that the world would stay lucky for ever. Hiroshima remained a grim warning of what the future could hold in store if humans failed to learn to resolve their conflicts peacefully.

HOW DID IT HAPPEN?

Nuclear peace

The fact that nuclear weapons have not been used since 1945 would have surprised many people alive at that time. The scientists who drafted the Franck Report (see page 21) believed that only 'international agreement on the future control of weapons' could avoid a catastrophic nuclear war. Manhattan Project scientist Leo Szilard felt that the use of the bombs against Japanese cities would make their future use in war even more likely. He wrote: 'Once they were introduced as an instrument of war it would be very difficult to resist the temptation of putting them to such use [again].'

However, Manhattan Project scientific director Robert Oppenheimer saw the atom bomb as the reason why a Third World War would not take place. He said: 'It did not take atomic weapons to make man want peace, a peace that would last. But the atomic bomb ... has made the prospect of future war unendurable.' It has also been argued that the use of the two bombs on Hiroshima and Nagasaki, by demonstrating the awfulness of their effect, deterred governments from using nuclear weapons again.

Szilard and Oppenheimer quoted in Richard Rhodes, *The Making of the Atomic Bomb* (Penguin, 1986)

Former Iraqi dictator Saddam Hussein is led away after being captured by US troops in December 2003. One of the declared objectives of the American-British invasion of Iraq was to stop Saddam from developing nuclear weapons.

Hiroshima Timeline

1937
7 July: Japanese invade China

1939
1 September: Second World War begins in Europe

October: Albert Einstein informs President Roosevelt of the possibility of making an atom bomb

1941
22 June: Nazi Germany invades the Soviet Union

7 December: The Japanese attack Pearl Harbor

December: Manhattan Project is set up in the United States to build an atom bomb

1942
15 February: The British base at Singapore surrenders to the Japanese

March: The United States begins moving Japanese Americans to camps

April: The Philippines fall to the Japanese

November: Los Alamos, New Mexico, is chosen as the hub of the Manhattan project

2 December: The first atomic chain reaction is achieved by scientists in Chicago

1944
September: Bomber Group 509 begins training to drop the atom bomb

October: Japanese pilots adopt kamikaze suicide tactics in attacks on the US fleet

1945
14 February: Dresden, Germany, is destroyed by Allied bombers

9–10 March: US firebomb raid destroys much of Tokyo

April–June: 12,500 US sevicemen are killed in the conquest of Okinawa

12 April: President Roosevelt dies; Harry S. Truman becomes president

8 May: Germany surrenders unconditionally to the Allies

June: Emperor Hirohito backs peace negotiations with the Allies

18 June: President Truman authorizes planning for an invasion of Japan, which is to take place on 1 November

16 July: The first atomic device is exploded at Alamogordo in New Mexico

17 July: The Potsdam Conference opens in the outskirts of Berlin

25 July: President Truman formally authorizes the use of atom bombs against Japan

26 July: The Allies call on Japan to surrender unconditionally in the Potsdam Declaration

28 July: Japanese government rejects Potsdam Declaration

6 August: An atom bomb is dropped on Hiroshima

8 August: The Soviet Union declares war on Japan

9 August: An atom bomb is dropped on Nagasaki

10 August: The Japanese say they will surrender if the emperor is allowed to keep his throne

14 August: The Japanese government informs the Allies that it is surrendering

15 August: Emperor Hirohito announces the country's surrender to the nation

2 September: The Japanese sign a formal surrender document

1949
September: The Soviet Union tests its first atom bomb

1952
April: Japan regains full independence

6 November: The United States explodes the first hydrogen bomb

1955
A Peace Museum and Peace Park open in Hiroshima

1962
October: The Cuban Missile Crisis brings the world to the brink of nuclear war

1991
25 December: The Soviet Union ceases to exist

Glossary

atom bomb A bomb in which an explosion is caused by nuclear fission – splitting the nuclei of atoms.

chain reaction A nuclear chain reaction happens when splitting one atomic nucleus releases particles that split other nuclei, and so on.

Cold War Period of tension between the United States and its allies and the Soviet Union and its allies, from the late 1940s to the late 1980s.

Communist A person who supports the political and economic system first established in the Soviet Union after 1917, involving rule by a single political party and state control of the economy.

gamma radiation Harmful radiation released in a nuclear explosion.

hydrogen bomb A bomb in which the explosion is produced by nuclear fusion – a process in which, rather than splitting apart, atomic nuclei unite with one another.

kamikaze In Japanese literally 'divine wind', a term used for pilots who carried out suicide attacks, deliberately crashing their aircraft into enemy ships.

militarist Person who believes the armed forces should dominate society and that warfare is the most important human activity.

Nazi The name of the political party, led by Adolf Hitler, that ruled Germany from 1933 to 1945.

nuclear fission Splitting of the nucleus of an atom, releasing energy and radiation.

nuclear reactor A device in which a controlled nuclear chain reaction is produced.

nuclear weapons Bombs, shells and missiles designed to produce explosions through nuclear fission or fusion.

nucleus The core of an atom (the plural is nuclei).

plutonium A metal found in small quantities in uranium ore, often used in nuclear reactors and nuclear weapons.

regime The government or governmental system of a country.

Soviet Union Country that included present-day Russia and 14 other republics. Ruled by the Soviet Communist Party, it disintegrated in 1991.

TNT Stands for trinitrotoluene, a high explosive.

unconditional surrender A total surrender, with no terms or conditions attached.

uranium A radioactive metal used as a source of nuclear energy and in some nuclear weapons.

warhead The part of a missile that carries the explosives.

Further Information

Books:

Alperovitz, Gar, *Atomic Diplomacy: Hiroshima and Potsdam* (Pluto Press, 1994)

Hershey, John, *Hiroshima* (latest edition Penguin, 2002)

Hogan, Michael (ed.), *Hiroshima in History and Memory* (Cambridge University Press, 1996)

Keegan, John, *The Second World War* (Pimlico, 1997)

McCullough, David, *Truman* (Simon and Schuster, 1993)

Rhodes, Richard, *The Making of the Atomic Bomb* (Penguin, 1986)

Walker, Stephen, *The Countdown to Hiroshima* (John Murray, 2005)

Wyden, Peter, *Day One: Before Hiroshima and After* (Warner Books, 1985)

Websites:

http://www.city.hiroshima.jp/index-E.html
http://www.csi.ad.jp/ABOMB
http://www.dannen.com/decision/index.html
http://www.inicom.com/hibakusha
http://www.theenolagay.com

Index
Numbers in **bold** refer to pictures